DEMONO|

CW01021075

TYPES OF DEMONS & ~~EVIL SPIRITS~~

Their Names & Activities
(Volume 11)

By

Michael Freze, S.F.O.

Copyright 2016 by Michael Freze, S.F.O.

Table of Contents

4

Spirits of Lying

Spirits of Seduction

Spirits of Wickedness

Spirits Who Deceive Nations

Worship of Demons

Activities Of The Evil Spirit

Poltergeist Phenomena

Diabolical Apparitions

Dedication

To all members of the Christian faith, who must face the powers of darkness on the journey to Christ. May you remain under God's grace and heed the words of St. Paul to the Ephesians:

Be strong in the Lord and in the strength of his might. Put on the whole armor of God, that you may be able to stand against the wiles of the devil. For we are not contending against flesh and blood, but against the principalities, against the powers, against the world rulers of this present darkness, against the spiritual hosts of wickedness in the heavenly places.Therefore take the whole armor of God, that you may be able to withstand in the evil day, and having done everything, to stand firm (6:10-13).

Acknowledgments

Any work that claims to have a single author is highly misleading and slightly less than honest. This work is no exception.

The truth of the matter is that all books regardless of the topic matter at hand are products of various sources and ideas that originate with different peoples in different places and times. Few ideas are new or original; many are just reworked or given a fresh perspective. This collective consciousness exists in all walks of life, although a few truly original ideas do appear from time to time.

Therefore, I acknowledge my indebtedness to the many sources that helped to make this book a reality. Any oversight on my part is purely unintentional. To all the unsung heroes who make up the collective consciousness of writers past and present, I extend my deepest appreciation.

To Father Patrick G. Patton of the Diocese of Helena, Montana: Thank you for continuing to support my writing career over the years. Father Patton provided encouragement and shared his insights for several of my past works. These include They Bore the Wounds of Christ: The Mystery of the Sacred Stigmata (1989) and The Making of Saints (1991), both published by Our Sunday Visitor.

To the Most Rev. Elden F. Curtiss, former Bishop of Helena and now Archbishop of Omaha: thank you for your encouragement concerning my writing apostolate. As the Ordinary of Helena, Bishop Curtiss was kind enough to take time out of his busy schedule to review this current work.

To Father Joseph Pius Martin, O.F.M. Cap., and Father Alessio Parente, O.F.M. Cap.: I am most grateful for your support and permission to use source materials from Our Lady of Grace Capuchin Friary in San Giovanni Rotondo, Italy. These two dear Capuchin friars have helped me with my past two works on the stigmata and the saints. Our meetings and interviews at the friary in 1988 and 1990 as well as our ongoing communications have led to a dear friendship that I will always cherish. Father Joseph and Father Alessio lived with the stigmatist Padre Pio (1887-1968) for a number of years before his death. Both served as his daily assistants and companions. Father Joseph Martin was present in Padre Pio's cell when he died.

To the dozens of authors, theologians, and saints throughout the years who have provided excellent works on this most complex of topics: Thank you. Without your previous exhaustive research and reflections, this work would not include the wisdom that you have imparted to all the faithful.

Preface

I decided from the beginning that this work would involve the study of demonology from a Catholic perspective but meant for all faiths. In no way does this book intend to discourage other faiths or denominations from studying its contents. Indeed, I made use
of a number of credible expert sources from non-Catholic traditions for some of my information. But by and large, I had decided to write this work principally from a Catholic perspective. Why?

For one thing, there are few recent works on demonology in the Catholic market that treat the topic in an in-depth, historical, and critical manner. The few works that do exist are usually focused upon one particular case, person, or phenomenon. Oftentimes these works are sensational in nature, a weakness I have tried to keep to a minimum.

Secondly, there are already many books on demonology in the Protestant markets. The Catholic market needs to devote some attention to this topic as well. Although there are many fine works on demonology in the Protestant field (indeed, it must be admitted that Protestant scholars have studied this phenomenon much more closely these past decades than Catholics as a whole). Nevertheless, there remains a serious drawback to most of these works in print.

Many of the popular works on demonology stem from fundamentalist and evangelical denominations. One of the problems associated with these works (at least for Catholics) is that they tend to emphasize a personal combat with evil forces that isolates these experiences from the authority and witness of the universal Church. Their Bible only theology and the personal relationship with God perspective separate the timeless, cosmic dimension of the spiritual warfare and also place this mystery of iniquity within the realm (and control) of private individuals who believe they possess a spiritual gift to cure all ills. To say that this fundamental, isolationist approach to the treatment of diabolical oppression or possession is wrong would be to understate the issue.

It must be clearly understood that the Catholic Church believes that the ongoing spiritual battle between the forces of darkness and light is essentially a cosmic conflict that only God can control through His own direct power or through the authority He commissions to His universal Church.

This Church, when acting under the name and authority of Jesus Christ, represents all true believers of the faith. In turn, some are appointed who have been delegated authority to act for the Church in a solemn, formal manner. This authoritative structure is
no small matter. Rather, the Church sees a special grace given to those ecclesiastical authorities who are considered successors of the original Apostles: namely, the bishops of the world. In turn, those the bishops appoint are given special graces to deal with the evil spirit in a confident, powerful manner.

Christ Himself promised special protection and power over the spirits of darkness for those whom He particularly calls: You did not choose me, but I chose you (Jn 15:16). In the Catholic Church, Christ commissions this work. He delegates His own authority through the ecclesiastical office of the Apostolic successors.

This chain of command or delegation of authority is precisely what is lacking in many fundamentalist and evangelical denominations. Yet Christ Himself makes is very clear that this is the will of God the Father. Even the Son is delegated authority through His Father: He who believes in me, believes not in me, but in him who sent me.. . . For I have not spoken on my own authority; the Father who sent me has himself given me commandment what to say and what to speak. And know that his commandment is eternal life. What I say, therefore, I say as the Father has bidden me (Jn 12:44-50).

In light of this revelation, it is difficult to understand how some of these religious groups justify their Bible only, personal relationship only positions concerning their faith life and theology. It is true that some are given personal charisms for particular benefits of the Church: Now there are a variety of gifts, but the same Spirit (1 Cor 12:4). But Jesus also taught us that when a special gift is used for the benefit of others in the universal Church, proper authority must be given to exercise such charisms in the name and authority of the Church: And he called to him his twelve disciples and gave them authority over unclean spirits, to cast them out, and to heal every disease and every infirmity (Mt 10:1; emphasis mine).

Oftentimes, many religious groups believe in their own authority through direct access to God; they do not subscribe to Apostolic succession or authority, nor do they believe in a hierarchical structure. Yet Jesus claimed that even in the world of faith, there indeed exists a hierarchical structure that all must respect: disciple is not above his teacher, nor a servant above his master; it is enough for the disciple to be like his teacher, and the servant like his master (Mt 10:24-25). Or again: He who receives you receives me, and he who receives me receives him who sent me (Mt 10:40).

Apostolic authority is as old as the Gospel itself. Yet many refuse to acknowledge such an authority! Jesus made the point clear in Matthew 16:18-19: And I tell you, you are Peter, and on this rock I will build my church, and the powers of death shall not prevail against it. I will give you the keys of the kingdom of heaven, and whatever you bind on earth shall be bound in heaven, and whatever you loose on earth shall be loosed in heaven.

Perhaps this explanation helps to clear up any misunderstandings that both Catholics and non-Catholics might have concerning the way the Church perceives her mission and duties regarding the battle against the evil spirit. It should be clear that there are fundamental differences in approaching the study of demonology between Catholics and others, especially in the actions taken against the evil spirit himself. Authority plays a crucial role in successfully dealing with the spirits of darkness, especially in the name and power of Jesus Christ. This we all can agree upon.

However, the Catholic Church believes that this very authority is not a private undertaking or venture. Rather, the authority of Jesus Christ is transmitted to others by virtue of the collective authority of the magisterium of the Church.

It is true that so-called deliverance prayer (a type of informal, private exorcism) is allowed to be practiced by certain Catholics experienced and knowledgeable in such matters. Indeed, we are all encouraged to resist the devil (Jas 4:7). This concerns efforts to combat demonic temptations, infiltrations, obsessions, etc. But for the more serious diabolical attacks such as with total oppression, partial possession, or complete possession deliverance prayer may not only be inadvisable; it may also be quite dangerous to the innocent victim who attempts to deal with the evil spirit on his or her own.

In such extreme situations, a formal exorcism may be in order. This type of expulsion of the evil spirit is a solemn public act, one that carries the authority of the universal Church behind it. It is Christ exercising His greatest power through His collective Body: The church is subject to Christ (Eph 5:24). St. Paul had pointed this out quite well: For the body does not consist of one member but many. . . Now you are the body of Christ and individually members of it (1 Cor 12:14, 27).

As far as understanding God's will, it is also through the authoritative structure of the Church that we find our best

teacher, director, and guide when combating the forces of darkness. It is dangerous to attempt a confrontation with the inhuman spirit without the aid of the collective wisdom and mighty grace of the Church: Through the church the manifold wisdom of God might now be made known to the principalities and powers in the heavenly places. This was according to the eternal purpose which he has realized in
Christ Jesus our Lord (Eph 3:10-11; emphasis mine).

Note that Paul does not restrict our God-given knowledge and powers to individuals for the sake of individuals; rather, God uses individual charisms through the authority of the Church for the benefit of its members. Anything other than that would be self-serving and could open the door for diabolical intervention and control.

Thus, with this preface I have intended to point out the different perspective one finds in the study of demonology from a Catholic point of view. As we have seen, this difference is important to note when considering the various theologies about demonology that exist throughout the Christian and non-Christian world.

This is not to say that the Catholic position is the only correct one; on the contrary, we all have much to learn from each other. But in any given field of study, one must start from a particular point of reference and remain true to the general principles of that particular view. Only then will one be able to express a viewpoint that is consistent and readily identifiable among the audience for which the work is intended. I hope that I have
achieved this purpose for the reader.

Introduction

Belief in the existence of the devil and various demonic forces has fascinated, mystified, and terrified the faithful since the beginning of human history. Despite what is sometimes called a morbid interest, little is known about the world of demonology except for the material gathered by those who have devoted themselves to studying this particular branch of spiritual theology. This usually includes various priests, nuns, theologians, mystics, saints, and Doctors of the Church.

Many have come to know the reality of the spirits of darkness through personal experience: those who have been oppressed or possessed, ecclesiastically appointed exorcists or their assistants, first-hand witnesses or victims of paranormal phenomena, etc.

What exactly is demonology? How does this term differ from other studies in the Christian faith? One thing that it is not is a practice that involves conjuring spirits, telecommunications, mental telepathy, psychic phenomena, seances, and so forth.

Although modern investigations do make use of other disciplines in the study of demonology, the above particular phenomena are subject to the scientific discipline known as paranormal psychology. (The use of parapsychology and all its aspects will be discussed at greater length later on in this work.)

Parapsychology is a field to be respected. I only wish to emphasize that these studies are used to help explain all phenomena that may not be the result of authentic diabolical activity. Thus, it is important to consider all disciplines that might reveal a natural or reasonable cause for actions too often presumed to be the work of the devil.

The main point is that although one studies and takes seriously these other fields such as parapsychology, no one encourages dabbling with the occult merely for curiosity. This must be kept in mind for all serious students involved with the modern study of demonology and all its ramifications.

To observe, study, and consider frequently requires a multidisciplinary approach. To perform experiments in the presence of experts (and with the proper permission and authority to do so!) is often necessary in order to identify a reasonable cause or effect.

Beyond that, it is a dangerous game to dabble with unseen forces or to attempt communications with spirits for the sake of innocent curiosity or amusement.

Above all, I want to set the record straight on this point: Do not do these things out of morbid curiosity! Leave this work to those experts who are commissioned by the authorities of the Church to do so. To ignore this advice is to open the door to potential danger.

Demonology may be defined as that theological discipline involving the study of all phenomena related to evil spirits: their creation, essence, substance, and interaction in the cosmic world. A demonologist studies the types and roles of evil spirits, their will, intelligence, power, and interaction with human beings. A demonologist is also concerned with the cosmic (or spiritual) battle between the forces of good and the forces of evil: the fall of Satan; the role of Michael the Archangel; the Antichrist; and the climactic encounter at the end of time.

This discipline examines preventive measures to use as protection against the spirits of darkness, as well as the treatments used for those already under attack from the evil spirit. Various signs and degrees of diabolical interaction are also dealt with in demonology: signs of temptation, infiltration, obsession, and oppression; deliverance prayer and ministry; informal and formal exorcism; and so forth.

Demonology may properly be called a specialized field of study within the discipline known as spiritual theology. This field must not be confused with angelology, which is reserved for the study of the heavenly angels: the archangels, the choirs of angels, guardian angels, and so on. Although both disciplines require an extensive understanding of all angelic creatures, nevertheless the primary focus of each one is separate and distinct.

Spiritual theology embraces a wide variety of specialized disciplines: demonology, angelology, prayer, spiritual direction, mystical theology, and aesthetic theology, to name but a few. Even moral theology may be considered so intimately bound to the spiritual or interior life that many consider this a sub-branch of spiritual theology.

Although the roots of demonology predate the existence of Christianity itself, our own century has witnessed a revival of interest in this mysterious topic. Indeed, the twentieth century as a whole and particularly the time since the early 1970s has been a period of revival unprecedented since the early Middle Ages. Particularly fascinating to some people today are the reported cases of possession and exorcism.

Although admittedly a rare phenomenon, diabolic possession has been a subject studied closely by the Catholic Church. Not so rare are the diabolical temptations, infiltrations, and even oppressions that continually plague the lives of individuals.

In order to deal with the cases of authentic oppression and possession that came before the Church throughout the centuries, it was agreed by Rome that there should be a formal, written guide as to the methods and procedures to be used concerning an authorized, formal exorcism. Created in 1614, this guide, known as the Rituale Romanum (Roman Ritual), was implemented during the pontificate of Pope Paul V

(1605-1621). The Rituale Romanum includes the rite of exorcism that each appointed exorcist uses.

Indeed, the Church takes this reality so seriously that she has even stated her formal position in the magisterial document of post-Vatican II: Les formes multiples de la superstition (Christian Faith and Demonology, Sacred Congregation for Divine Worship, June 26, 1975).

On November 15, 1972, in his General Address, Pope Paul VI had this to say about the reality of the spirits of darkness: Evil is not merely the lack of something, but an effective agent, a living, spiritual being, perverted and perverting. A terrible reality. Mysterious and frightening. It is contrary to the teaching of the Bible and the Church to refuse to recognize the existence of such a reality. . . , or to explain it as a pseudo-reality, a conceptual and fanciful personification of the unknown causes of our misfortunes. The Devil was a murderer from the beginning . . . and the father of lies, as Christ defines him (John 8:44-45); he launches sophistic attacks on the moral equilibrium of man. . . .

Not that every sin is directly attributable to diabolical action; but it is true that those who do not watch over themselves with a certain moral strictness (cf. Mt 12:45; Eph 6:11) are exposed to the influence of the `mysterium iniquitatis' to which St. Paul refers (2 Thes 2:3-12) and run the risk of being damned (L'Osservatore Romano, November 23, 1972).

The cause of such revival is not too difficult to detect. In our modern era of television, radio, and the print media, the sensational topics are accessible to every home throughout the civilized world. Curiosity provided by a massive influx through the media begins a wave of interest that then sustains itself. Another factor contributing to the recent interest concerning the devil or demons is the obsession with Satanism and witchcraft. This interest has increased dramatically throughout the world.

Oftentimes, members of these cults identify with drugs and alcohol, which further influence their imaginations and contribute to their lack of inhibitions. This is particularly true in those areas of life that call for moral decisions and actions that normally guide our thoughts and conscience as individuals and as a society. Drugs can alter those inhibitive feelings, opening up the door to innocent exploring and dabbling with the occult. Naturally, this produces an invitation for diabolical intrusion at some deeper point of one's involvement.

Satanism, sorcery, witchcraft, black magic these have all been with us for centuries. Yet the increased use of psychoactive-psychedelic drugs is at an all-time high, creating a virtual cesspool of naive and confused people who look for something bigger and better in order to find meaning and fulfillment in their lives. Drugs and alcohol can be effective catalysts for those who are young, confused, and curious. They can also be open invitations to the lures of the devil.

Anton LaVey, founder and high priest of San Francisco's First Church of Satan, once claimed that the Satanic Age began in 1966. His own books, The Satanic Bible (1969) and The Satanic Rituals (1972), both published by Avon Books, have sold in the thousands. And no wonder. Statistics report that in France alone there are more than sixty thousand sorcerers earning two hundred thousand dollars per year for their services. In another report, it was said that six thousand witches meet on a regular basis to perform their rituals in England.

Perhaps the most influence regarding modern-day fascination with demonology is generated through books and through television. The real mass, or popular, revival concerning an interest in demonology began with the William P. Blatty novel The Exorcist (first published in 1971). Although the novel used a twelve-year-old girl named Regan MacNeil as the possessed victim of the story, this novel was based upon the real-life story of Douglass Deen, a thirteen-year-old possessed boy from the Washington, D.C., suburb of Mount Rainier. Deen allegedly experienced a number of poltergeist phenomena between January and May of 1949; he was also the victim of obscene diabolical gestures, physical attacks, obsession, and complete possession.

It is claimed that the Deens' Lutheran pastor attempted to free the boy from diabolical attacks but to no avail. After accompanying the boy through unsuccessful medical and psychiatric evaluations at Georgetown Hospital and at the hospital at St. Louis University (both Jesuit institutions), the Jesuits took official control of the situation.

In due time, Deen was helped by a Jesuit priest in his fifties. This priest was formally commissioned by the Church to perform the exorcism. Although the exorcism was successful, it took thirty separate attempts over a six-month period to complete the ordeal. The exorcist eventually retired in St. Louis. In a strange twist of fate, Douglass Deen like William Peter Blatty attended Georgetown University. He later married and raised a family. In 1949, this extraordinary story was well-known to William Peter Blatty, a Catholic student at Georgetown University in Washington, D.C. He would live with this experience for several decades before committing his story to print.

Following the phenomenal success of the book, The Exorcist was made into a movie (1972). Its director, William Friedkin, once interviewed the seventy-two-year-old aunt of the boy who was eventually exorcised of his demons. On August 27, 1972, The New York Times reviewed the film. The reviewer, Chris Chase, interviewed Douglass Deen's aunt concerning the real story behind the movie. Many terrifying phenomena were explained in that interview: poltergeist activity, shaking beds, a mattress that rose in the air, etc. According to the aunt, this all occurred one day when Douglass Deen had visited her home before the exorcism.

Another film that opened the doors of public curiosity is Rosemary's Baby, a 1966 motion picture that depicts a young actor who makes a pact with a group of Satanists. In turn, this group is given permission to use the actor's wife as the bride of Satan in order that evil might be introduced into the world. As a reward for such sacrifices, the young actor is promised wealth and success.

More recently, a book called The Amityville Horror by Jay Anson rocked the nation with its story of a terrorized family (the Lutzes) who live in a possessed Long Island home. Apparently, the house was originally built on an Indian burial ground. Having been disturbed in the past, it is claimed that demonic spirits took over the residence. It is also claimed that in the late 1600s, John Ketchum, expelled from Salem, Massachusetts, for practicing witchcraft, lived on the spot where this 1928 Dutch Colonial home now stands. In November of 1974, a story reports that twenty-two-year-old Ronald DeFeo killed his entire family with a .35 caliber rifle in this house, claiming that Satan made him do it. All told, Ronald's parents, his two brothers, and two sisters died that night.

From December 18, 1975, to January 7, 1976, George and Kathy Lutz lived in the haunted home. The Lutzes experienced a multitude of paranormal phenomena from unseen forces, including the following: poltergeist activity; foul smells throughout the house; demonic visions; scratchings in the walls; unexplained temperature changes; cold spots in the house; blood oozing from the walls; and violent, physical attacks from unseen forces. Needless to say, the Lutzes left their new home after only twenty days.

Dozens of parapsychologists, scientists, and ecclesiastical figures investigated the home; extensive interviews were also held with the Lutzes. The story remains controversial, as some of the experts confirm the authenticity of the reported events and some do not. Since that time, a number of Amityville sequels have hit the markets. Several successful movies have been made from the original books as well.

It is obvious that such media coverage attracts public attention and causes unprecedented interest in such reported cases. Although a great deal of these stories are sensationalized, many are certainly not true; nevertheless it must be acknowledged that some of them have to be authentic. There have been too many of these paranormal experiences reported to dismiss them outright. There is simply too much credible evidence from professional authorities (not to mention countless eyewitnesses) who swear by the observations they have experienced.

In light of this fact, the reader needs to keep an open mind about such reported incidences. A healthy approach is a cautious one: Doubt each case until the evidence is very convincing, but do not deny every reported incident out of hand. This would be a tragic mistake, for the Church demands that we believe in the reality of Satan, the demons, and their ability to interact in our lives.

The evil spirit would love nothing more than for the faithful to believe that he does not exist. The devil tries to disguise his actions lest he be caught. To ruin the lives of many and to capture souls away from the kingdom of God without being acknowledged allows him to carry on his tactics unopposed. Remember the words of St. Paul: Even Satan disguises himself as an angel of light (2 Cor 11:14).

One final thing: It cannot be emphasized enough that many of the supernatural apparitions and messages contained in this work have not yet received official approval of the Church, and are still under ecclesiastical investigation. Therefore, the reader must realize that these claims are not necessarily the beliefs or opinions of the author or publisher, nor are they intended to be an official position of the Church.

Demonic Spirits

Names of the Evil Spirit

The word devil comes from the Greek diabolos, which is also known as (Italian), diablo (Spanish), and diable (French). In all languages, the original meaning of this word translates as accuser or traitor.

In translating the Old Testament into Greek, the Egyptian Jews of the third century used the word diabolos for the Hebrew satan, an angelic entity whose function was to test man's fidelity to God. He was not evil but became evil by identification with his functions. Thus satan was given power to inflict sufferings on Job (Jb 1:6-12; see 1 Chr 21:1). When this Greek Septuagint Old Testament was turned into Latin, diabolos became either diabolus (in the early translations) or Satan (in the standard Vulgate text).

In the New Testament, however, the Greek word satanas was used to mean something very different, not an adversary against man (as in Job), but an adversary against God, as employed by Christ at the temptation on the mountain: Begone, Satan! (Mt 4:10). Throughout the New Testament, Satanas meant the devil, and in Revelation 12:9 was described as the great dragon . . . that ancient serpent, who is called the Devil and Satan, the deceiver of the whole world.

In the English translations, the Old Testament Hebrew satan as well as the New Testament Greek satanas were, following the Latin, both rendered Satan.

Scripture has given us ample evidence of the reality of the spirits of darkness, as we can readily see from the references given below. Here are some of the many descriptive names referring to the devil in both the Old and New Testaments:

Abaddon (Rv 9:11).

Accuser of our brothers (Rv 12:10).

Adversary (1 Tm 5:14; 1 Pt 5:8).

Angel of light (2 Cor 11:14).

Angel of the bottomless pit (Rv 9:11).

Anointed cherub (Ez 28:14).

Apollyon (Greek) (Rv 9:11).

Beelzebub (Mt 10:25, 12:27; Mk 3:22; Lk 11:15, 18-19).

Belial (Dt 13:13; Jgs 19:22, 20:13: 1 Sm 1:16, 2:12,

10:27, 25:17, 25, 30:22; 2 Sm 16:7, 20:1, 23:6).

Covering cherub (Ez 28:16).

Enemy (Ps 17:4).

Dragon (Rv 12:4, 7, 13, 16-17, 13:2, 4, 16:13, 20:2).

Evil one (Mt 6:13, 13:19; Jn 17:15; 1 Jn 2:13, 5:18).

God of this world (2 Cor 4:4).

Huge dragon (Rv 12:3, 9).

Liar (Jn 8:44).

Lying spirit (1 Kgs 22:22, 23).

Master of the house (Mt 10:25).

Morning star (Is 14:12).

Murderer (Jn 8:44).

Old serpent (Rv 12:9, 20:2).

Prince of the demons (Mt 9:34; Mk 3:22).

Prince of the power of the air (Eph 2:2).

Prince of this world (Jn 12:31, 14:20, 16:11).

Serpent (Gn 3:1, 2, 4, 13, 14; 2 Cor 11:3; Rv 12:14-15).

Son of the dragon (Is 14:12).

Tempter (Mt 4:3; 1 Thes 3:5).

Thief (Jn 10:10).

Unclean spirit (Mt 12:43; Mk 3:30; Lk 9:42).

The Sacred Scriptures overwhelmingly support the existence of an evil force that is preternatural and an enemy to all of mankind.

What characteristics do the demons have that make them so feared and detested by the saints and mystics of all ages? The Scriptures are full of examples depicting the nature and activities of the devil and his cohorts:

Accuser (Rv 12:10).

Anger (Mk 9:20, 26; Acts 19:16).

Antagonistic (Mt 8:29; Mk 1:24; Acts 19:16; Rv 2:10).

Beguiler (Gn 3:13).

Betrayer (Jn 13:2).

Blasphemer (Rv 2:9).

Crazy (Mt 17:15).

Deceitful (Mt 13:19; Lk 8:12; Jn 10:10; 1 Tm 4:1;

2 Tm 3:13; 1 Jn 4:1; Rv 12:9, 13:14, 20:3, 8).

Dishonest (Jn 10:10).

Hypocritical (1 Tm 4:2).

Jealous (Nm 5:14, 30).

Liar (1 Kgs 22:22-23; Mt 13:22; Jn 8:44; Acts 5:3;

2 Thes 2:9; 1 Tm 4:2).

Loud (Mk 1:26).

Lustful (Jn 8:44).

Mean (Mt 8:29).

Murderer (Jn 8:44).

Revengeful (1 Pt 5:8).

Seducer (1 Tm 4:1; 2 Tm 3:13).

Tempter (Mt 4:1, 3; Lk 4:2, 13; 1 Cor 7:5;

1 Tm 4:1).

Troublesome (Mt 13:39).

Vain (Ez 28:17).

Vexed (Mt 15:22, 17:15; Lk 6:18; Acts 5:16).

Violent (Mt 17:15; Mk 1:26, 9:20, 26; Acts 8:7, 19:16;

1 Pt 5:8).

Wicked (Mt 12:45; Lk 11:26).

The Sacred Scriptures are only a small source of the names that refer to the devils or demons of the world. In the practice of Satanism and witchcraft, there are literally hundreds of diabolical names that are called upon for favors, wisdom, spells, etc. It appears that many practitioners believe in a hierarchy of devils and demons, each with specific duties, abilities, and powers. One such example can be found in what is known as The Infernal Names, a list of various evil spirits who are summoned for specific favors:

Abaddon (Hebrew): the destroyer.

Adramelech: Samaritan devil.

Ahpuch: Mayan devil.

Ahriman: Mazdean devil.

Amon: Egyptian ram-headed god of life and reproduction.

Apollyon: Greek synonym for Satan, the archfiend.

Asmodeus: Hebrew devil of sensuality and luxury.

Astaroth: Phoenician goddess of lasciviousness.

Azazel (Hebrew): taught man to make weapons of war.

Baalberith: Canaanite Lord of the covenant who was later made a devil.

Balaam: Hebrew devil of avarice and greed.

Baphomet: worshiped by the Templars as symbolic of Satan.

Bast: Egyptian goddess of pleasure represented by the cat.

Beelzebub (Hebrew): Lord of the Flies, taken from symbolism of the scarab.

Behemoth: Hebrew personification of Satan in the form of an elephant.

Beherit: Syriac name for Satan.

Bile: Celtic god of hell.

Chemosh: national god of Moabites, later a devil.

Cimeries: rides a black horse and rules Africa.

Coyote: American Indian devil.

Dagon: Philistine avenging devil of the sea.

Damballa: voodoo serpent god.

Demogorgon: Greek name for the devil, it is said it should not be known to mortals.

Diabolus (Greek): flowing downward.

Dracula: Romanian name for devil.

Emma-O: Japanese ruler of hell.

Euronymous: Greek prince of death.

Fenriz: son of Loki, depicted as a wolf.

Gorgo: diminutive of Demogorgon, Greek name for the devil.

Haborym: Hebrew synonym for Satan.

Hecate: Greek goddess of the underworld and witchcraft.

Ishtar: Babylonian goddess of fertility.

Kali (Hindu): daughter of Shiva, high priestess of the Thuggees.

Lilith: Hebrew female devil, Adam's first wife who taught him the ropes.

Loki: (Teutonic) devil.

Mammon: Aramaic god of wealth and profit.

Mania: Etruscan goddess of hell.

Mantus: Etruscan god of hell.

Marduk: god of the city of Babylon.

Mastema: Hebrew synonym for Satan.

Melek Taus: Yezidi devil.

Mephistopheles (Greek): he who shuns the light.

Metztli: Aztec goddess of the night.

Mictian: Aztec god of death.

Midgard: son of Loki, depicted as a serpent.

Milcom: Ammonite devil.

Moloch: Phoenician and Canaanite devil.

Mormo (Greek): King of the Ghouls, consort of Hecate.

Naamah: Hebrew female devil of seduction.

Nergal: Babylonian god of Hades.

Nihasa: American Indian devil.

Nija: Polish god of the underworld.

O-Yama: Japanese name for Satan.

Pan: Greek god of lust, later relegated to devildom.

Pluto: Greek god of the underworld.

Prosperpine: Greek queen of the underworld.

Pwcca: Welsh name for Satan.

Rimmon: Syrian devil worshiped at Damascus.

Sabazios: Phrygian origin, identified with Dionysos, snake worship.

Saitan: Enochian equivalent of Satan.

Sammael (Hebrew): venom of God.

Samnu: Central Asian devil.

Sedit: American Indian devil.

Sekhmet: Egyptian goddess of vengeance.

Set: Egyptian devil.

Shaitan: Arabic name for Satan.

Shiva (Hindu): the destroyer.

Supay: Inca god of the underworld.

T'an-mo: Chinese counterpart to the devil, covetousness, desire.

Tchort: Russian name for Satan, black god.

Tezcatlipoca: Aztec god of hell.

Thamuz: Sumerian god who later was relegated to devildom.

Thoth: Egyptian god of magic.

Tunrida: Scandinavian female devil.

Typhon: Greek personification of Satan.

Yaotzin: Aztec god of hell.

Yen-lo-Wang: Chinese ruler of hell.

Devils and Demons

In the New Testament, the term devil has the same general meaning as demon. Demon comes from the Latin word daemon, which in effect means evil spirit. In turn, demon or demonic spirit comes from the Greek daimonion, which is the diminutive of daimon, referring to a god or spirit. In six other places in the New Testament, these demons are called pondera, which means evil spirits, and in twenty-three references they are known as akatharta (unclean spirits).

Although it is often thought that a devil is none other than Satan and Satan indeed is a devil. Nevertheless there are cohorts (helpers) of Satan that have a hierarchical structure, similar to that which is found with the angels of heaven: the Seraphim (Is 6:1), the Cherubim (Gn 3:23; Ex 25:18; Ps 79:2, 98:1), the Thrones (Col 1:16), the Dominions (Col 1:16), the Virtues (Eph 1:21), the Powers (Dn 3:61; Eph 3:10), the Principalities (Rom 8:38: Eph 3:10; Col 1:16), the Archangels (Nm 13:13; Tb 3-12; Dn 8:16, 9:21, 10:13, 21; 1 Thes 4:16; Jude 1:9; Rv 12:7), and the Angels (hundreds of Old and New Testament references from Genesis through Revelation).

Likewise, the diabolic hierarchical structure is also in evidence: At the top of the powers of the spirits of darkness is Satan (Lucifer or the devil); under Satan's authority are other devils who help to carry out Satan's attacks; finally, the lesser evil spirits are known as demons. In turn, the demons consist of higher spirits and those known as familiars: demons of lesser intelligence and power that are attracted to particular people and who act on behalf of higher demonic spirits. In effect, familiars serve as diabolical proxies for greater and more powerful demons who themselves are acting on behalf of other devils or Satan.

Characteristics of the Evil Spirit

Inhuman Spirits

The demonic spirits, like all the angelic creatures made by God, are incorporeal entities; that is, they lack a physical or material nature. The incorporeality of living spiritual beings and their subsequent distinction from corporeal realities is firmly rooted in Sacred Scripture. In the Gospel of Luke, the Evangelist describes this very point. When the disciples were gathered together in Jerusalem, the risen Lord appeared to them in his supernatural bodily form. Thinking that He was a spirit (24:37), Jesus' followers heard Him make this statement: spirit has not flesh and bones as you see that I have (Lk 24:39).

In Matthew's Gospel, Jesus was visiting the home of Peter's mother-in-law. There, many came who were possessed with demons; and he cast out the spirits with a word, and healed all who were sick (Mt 8:16). The Evangelist Mark records the following: And when Jesus saw that a crowd came running together, he rebuked the unclean spirit, saying to it, `You dumb and deaf spirit, I command you, come out of him, and never enter him again' (Mk 9:25). St. Paul once referred to the demons as spiritual hosts of wickedness (Eph 6:12), and St. John had visions of demonic spirits who do battle with the followers of Christ (Rv 16:14).

Although angelic or demonic spirits are incorporeal in nature, nevertheless they are able to take on physical, observable characteristics from time to time in order to communicate with human beings. This is evident in the Book of Acts, where Peter and Paul saw and talked with an angel (see Acts 5:19, 27:23-24). The physical manifestation of angelic beings is used in order to teach, counsel, warn, to send messages, or to deliver favors for the one who experiences such a phenomenon. With demonic spirits, the manifestation occurs in order to threaten, frighten, or confuse a victim of diabolical intervention.

Other teachings about incorporeal beings are found in the Bible as well. The Apostle Paul claims that we all will take on spiritual bodies when we pass to eternal life: Lo! I tell you a mystery. We shall not all sleep, but we shall all be changed, in a moment, in the twinkling of an eye, at the last trumpet. For the trumpet will sound, and the dead will be raised imperishable, and this perishable nature must put on the imperishable, and this mortal nature must put on immortality (1 Cor 15:51-53). A bit earlier in the same work, St. Paul tells us that flesh and blood cannot inherit the kingdom of God (1 Cor 15:50).

Paul is referring to the resurrection of our human bodies, which, like Christ's, will be glorified. The point is clear: There is another level of reality in the eternal order that is spiritual in nature and infinitely more perfect than the present, physical condition.

Although demonic spirits can hardly be called beautiful or perfect, we must remember that they are of the same essence and substance as their heavenly counterparts the archangels, heavenly hosts, and guardian angels of the created order. Lest we forget, it must be stated that every diabolical spirit is in essence a created spirit of equal order and being as the heavenly angels that God has created. This was so in the beginning before Satan and his cohorts rebelled against God and were cast down from heaven. Free will and the choice of good or evil does not change the fundamental essence or substance of the created being. The same wisdom, majesty, intelligence, and power remain in all that is created.

Thus, to imply that demonic spirits are inferior to the heavenly angels in these areas or that they now possess inferior abilities or characteristics as their counterparts would be a mistake in judgment. Outside of St. Michael the Archangel, Satan still retains the same wisdom, intelligence, and power as the greatest and loftiest of the heavenly angels. These characteristics have not disappeared nor have they been lessened: only misdirected in all their fullness toward evil designs.

This being the case, it would be foolish indeed to challenge the diabolical spirit, for it is much more ancient, far more wise and powerful than any physical creature on this planet. Only through the help and protection of God the Father, Jesus our Lord, the Blessed Virgin Mary, Michael the Archangel, the saints, and our guardian angels can we hope to defeat the forces of darkness.

In union with the authority of the Church (which in herself is acting on the power and authority of Christ Jesus), the spirits of darkness will meet their challenge. For those foolish enough to go it alone, a certain defeat physical, emotional, spiritual, and psychological is almost a foregone conclusion.

What is the very essence of inhumanness? It is the absence of every quality, characteristic, and condition that makes us what we are beautiful people created in God's image (Gn 1:26), sharers in the divine nature through the grace of Jesus Christ: Whoever confesses that Jesus is the Son of God, God abides in him, and he in God (1 Jn 4:15).

Inhumanness is the total rejection of all that is God: faith, hope, love, truth, and righteousness: If you love me, you will keep my commandments (Jn 14:15). Moreover, it is the denial and unbelief in Jesus (1 Jn 2:22), and the rejection of redemption and eternal salvation in Christ: Every spirit which does not confess Jesus is not of God. This is the spirit of antichrist (1 Jn 4:3); it is the lack of charity and compassion toward humanity: I was hungry and you gave me food, I was thirsty and you gave me drink, I was a stranger and you welcomed me, I was naked and you clothed me, I was sick and you visited me, I was in prison and you came to see me (Mt 25:35-36).

The evil spirit, opposed to all that is true and good namely, God and His created beings hates everything that reflects the image of the divine. Hence, the demonic spirit will do anything possible to corrupt God's creation and bring it to its ruin. We know from the testimony of the Scriptures that human beings are destined for eternal life and salvation: And this is the testimony, that God gave us eternal life, and this life is in his Son (1 Jn 5:11).

Thus, it is the very substance of immortality that the evil one seeks to destroy: the human spirit, that breath of divine life (Gn 2:7). To be human is to reject all that God is not. To remain human is to live the life of the Gospel (1 Cor 9:14), to follow God's commandments (Jn 14:15), to absorb the way of the beatitudes (Mt 5:1-17), to love God with all our hearts (Mk 12:30), and to show charity and compassion for our neighbor: You shall love your neighbor as yourself (Mk 12:31). These are the weapons to use against the spirits of darkness, to retain our human dignity. Without them, eternal damnation lies closely in the hands of the enemy.

Types Of Evil Spirits

There are numerous types of evil spirits that influence humanity. It seems clear that these spirits are given certain roles and duties to assist in the works of the devil.

The demoniacal hierarchy made up of Satan, the devils, and various types of demons, which involves the levels of power and authority in the demonic world is also broken down into categories of demon-types that attack a victim at his weakest link: physical problems, emotional disturbances, psychological imbalances, spiritual weaknesses, obsessive and compulsive tendencies, aggressive behavior, sexual urges, dreams and fantasies, material desires, etc.

Though they are pure spirit, these demon-types appear to have separate and distinct personalities. This should not surprise us, for we know that the evil spirit has remarkable intelligence and unusual characteristics.

Because of the fact that humans are distinct in their own way, particular demons are attracted to specific persons according to their physical, psychological, and spiritual dispositions. Thus, what attracts one type of demon to a certain individual may not be the case with another (even two people in the same home may not be tempted or oppressed in the same manner).

Sacred Scripture gives many examples of individual spirits as well as multiple spirits who intervene in the cause of human affairs. This is true for both Old Testament and New Testament texts. In fact, angelic beings are mentioned in the Bible directly or indirectly some three hundred times.

The ability for many spirits to act in our lives simultaneously should not be surprising, for the Bible teaches that there are innumerable spiritual beings that exist in the created order (see Heb 12:22).

How do we know such things? Are there really thousands of such creatures that live among us? The Book of Deuteronomy gives us a clue: The Lord came from Sinai, and dawned from Seir upon us; he shone forth from Mount Paran, he came from the ten thousands of holy ones, with flaming fire at his right hand (Dt 33:2).

In Psalms, the prophet describes angelic beings in the symbolic imagery of chariots. Here, too, a vast number of such beings is described: With mighty chariotry, twice ten thousand, thousands upon thousands, the Lord came from Sinai into the holy place (Ps 68:17). This passage cannot adequately describe how many angels there really are. Perhaps the number is in the millions; this we can never know.

In the New Testament, several verses speak in a similar fashion: Then I looked, and I heard around the throne and the living creatures and the elders the voice of many angels, numbering myriads and thousands of thousands, saying with a loud voice, `Worthy is the Lamb who was slain, to receive power and wealth and wisdom and might and honor and glory and blessing!' (Rv 5:11-12). Of course, a myriad is ten thousand. Multiple myriads may imply a number so enormous that millions are involved.

The Apostle John was overcome by such a vast number of angelic beings in existence that he used clouds as his symbolic representation for their presence at the return of Christ: Behold, he is coming with the clouds, and every eye will see him (Rv 1:7). If every human eye will witness this phenomenon, their number must be great, indeed! Although many may discredit this image because of the symbolism throughout Revelation, Paul reveals this same fact, where he describes the Lord's coming from heaven with his mighty angels in flaming fire (2 Thes 1:7).

Although we may know that this is true for the heavenly angels, it is equally true for those who have fallen. Demonic spirits are innumerable as well: Their number is like the sand of the sea (Rv 20:7-8). It is a frightening thought that perhaps as Scripture implies thirty-three percent of them are close to the human environment: And another portent appeared in heaven; behold, a great red dragon, with seven heads and ten horns, and seven diadems around his heads. His tail swept down a third of the stars of heaven, and cast them down to earth. . . . And the great dragon was thrown down, that ancient serpent, who is called the Devil and Satan, the deceiver of the whole world he was thrown down to the earth, and his angels were thrown down with him (Rv 12:3-4, 9). If John gives an accurate description of these fallen spirits, then literally thousands of them prowl around like a roaring lion, seeking someone to devour (1 Pt 5:8). Why are evil spirits allowed to interfere with the goodness of God's creation? We will never know in this lifetime, for St. Paul describes this as the mystery of lawlessness (2 Thes 2:7).

Perhaps the demonic spirits are not strictly limited to our earthly environment. Scripture would seem to indicate otherwise. Are some evil spirits allowed to remain in heaven or to appear there from time to time? St. Paul indicates that this might be the case: For we are not contending against flesh and blood, but against the principalities, against the powers, against the world rulers of this present darkness, against the spiritual hosts of wickedness in the heavenly places (Eph 6:12).

It also seems apparent that demons exist at the same time in a real, tormenting place called hell (Gehenna), an eternal place of fire and punishment for all who reject the living God: But I will warn you whom to fear: fear him who, after he has killed, has power to cast into hell; yes, I tell you, fear him! (Lk 12:5);Then he will say to those at his left hand, `Depart from me, you cursed, into the eternal fire prepared for the devil and his angels' (Mt 25:41).

Another passage supports this position: And the angels that did not keep their own position but left their proper dwelling have been kept by him in eternal chains in the nether gloom until the judgment of the great day (Jude 6). Yet it also might be that hell will not contain demonic spirits until after the last judgment when Christ returns. This implication is given in the Gospel: Then he will say to those at his left hand, `Depart from me, you cursed, into the eternal fire prepared for the devil and his angels' (Mt 25:41). Whether or not the spirits of darkness are currently in hell as well as on this earth is hard to say, based upon these seemingly conflicting statements.

Views of Demonologists

Demonologist Alphonsus de Spina (Fortalicium Fidei)
concluded that there were ten types of devils:

1. Fates
Some say they have seen Fates, but if so they are not women
but demons (and Augustine says the only fate is the will of
God).

2. Poltergeists

Also known as duende de casa, these noisy spirits or ghosts
have been known to be involved in various and unusual
phenomena: throwing things in the air, causing items to break
or explode, starting fires spontaneously, making footsteps
overhead, pulling off bedclothes, etc.

3. Incubi and Succubi

These are demons that sexually molest their victims. Nuns are
especially prone to these devils. When they awake in the
morning, they find themselves polluted as if they had slept
with men.

4. Marching hosts
These appear like hordes of men making much tumult.

5. Familiar demons

Ä These eat and drink with men, in imitation of the angel Tobit.

6. Nightmare demons

Ä These terrify men in their dreams.

7. Fertility demons

Formed from semen and its odor when men and women copulate, these also cause men to dream of women so the demons can receive their emission and make therefrom a new spirit. (Spina did not believe this.)

8. Deceptive demons

These sometimes appear as men and sometimes as women.

9. Clean demons

Called clean but really quite foul, these assail only holy men.

10. Deceiving demons

These deceive old women (called xorguinae or bruxae).

In another study of demonic types and classifications, demonologist Francesco-Maria Guazzo in his Compendium Maleficarum explained that there are six varieties of demons, depending upon their habitation. Here is the list Guazzo had quoted from an earlier work by Michaelis Psellus (De Operatione Daemonum Dialogus):

1. The first is the fiery, because these dwell in the upper air and will never descend to the lower regions until the Day of Judgment, and they have no dealings on earth with men.

2. The second is the aerial, because these dwell in the air around us. They can descend to hell, and, by forming bodies out of the air, can at times be visible to men. Very frequently, with God's permission, they agitate the air and raise storms and tempests, and all this they conspire to do for the destruction of mankind.

3. The third is terrestrial, and these were certainly cast from heaven to earth for their sins. Some of them live in the woods and forests, and lay snares for hunters; some dwell in the fields and lead night travelers astray; some dwell in hidden places and caverns; while others delight to live in secret among men.

4. The fourth is the aqueous, for these dwell under the water in river and lakes, and are full of anger, turbulent, unquiet, and deceitful. They raise storms at sea, sink ships in the ocean, and destroy life in the water. When such devils appear, they are more often women than men, for they live in moist places and lead an easier life. But those that live in drier and harder places are usually seen as males.

5. The fifth is the subterranean, for these live in caves and caverns in the mountains. They are of a very mean disposition, and chiefly molest those who work in pits or mines for treasure, and they are always ready to do harm. They cause earthquakes and winds and fires, and shake the foundations of houses.

6. The sixth is the heliophobic, because they especially hate and detest the light, and never appear during the daytime, nor can they assume a bodily form until night. These devils are completely inscrutable and of a character beyond human comprehension, because they are all dark within, shaken with icy passions, malicious, restless, and perturbed; and when they meet men at night they oppress them violently and, with God's permission, often kill them by some breath or touch. . . . This kind of devil has no dealing with witches; neither can they be kept at bay by charms, for they shun the light and the voices of men and every sort of noise.

Demonic Hierarchy

In the Middle Ages, many demonologists attempted to identify devils and demons according to their hierarchical structure. One such attempt placed the demons according to their relationship with the seven deadly sins: **Lucifer** (pride); **Mammon** (avarice); **Asmodeus** (lechery); **Satan** (anger); **Beelzebub** (gluttony); **Leviathan** (envy); and **Belphegor** (sloth) (Tractatus de Confessionibus Maleficorum et Sagarum).

Sacred Scripture reveals that there indeed are numerous diabolical spirits who are classified according to devils and demons: Then he will say to those at his left hand, `Depart from me, you cursed, into the eternal fire prepared for the devil and his angels' (Mt 25:41).

Furthermore, we see in another verse that there are degrees of demonic powers throughout the universe: For we are not contending against flesh and blood, but against the principalities, against the powers, against the world rulers of this present darkness, against the spiritual hosts of wickedness in the heavenly places (Eph 6:12).

The angelic court had been invented in the fourth century, out of the writings of St. Paul (Col 1:16; Eph 1:21), by the Pseudo-Dionysius, and consisted of nine orders of angels (three hierarchies each of three orders): **First Hierarchy** (seraphim, cherubim, thrones); **Second Hierarchy** (dominions, principalities, powers); and **Third Hierarchy** (virtues, archangels, angels).

A Father Sebastian Michaelis in his work Histoire admirable de la possession et conversion d'une penitente gave a detailed account of these three hierarchical orders:

First Hierarchy

Beelzebub was Prince of the Seraphim, and next unto Lucifer. For all the princes, that is to say all the chief of nine choirs of angels, are fallen; and of the choir of Seraphim there fell the three first, to wit, Lucifer, Beelzebub, and Leviathan, who did all revolt. But the fourth, who was Michael, was the first that resisted Lucifer, and all the rest of those good angels followed him, so that now he is the chiefest amongst them all. Lucifer, when Christ descended into hell, was there chained up, where he commands all. . . . Beelzebub tempts men with pride. And as John the Baptist holds Lucifer's place in Paradise . . . by his singular humility, so Beelzebub has Francis for his adversary in heaven.

Leviathan is the Prince of the same order, and is the ringleader of the heretics, tempting men with sins that are directly repugnant unto faith. (Adversary: Peter the Apostle.)

Asmodeus is of the same order. He continues a Seraphim to this day, that is, he burns with the desire to tempt men with his swine of luxuriousness, and is the prince of wantons. (Adversary: John the Baptist.)

Balberith is Prince of the Cherubim. He tempts men to commit homicides, and to be quarrelsome, contentious, and blasphemous. (Adversary: Barnabas.)

Astaroth, Prince of the Thrones, is always desirous to sit idle and be at ease. He tempts men with idleness and sloth. (Adversary: Bartholomew.)

Verrine is also one of the Thrones, and next in place unto Astaroth, and tempts men with impatience. (Adversary: Dominic.)

Gressil is the third in the order of Thrones, and tempts men with impurity and uncleanliness. (Adversary: Bernard.)

Sonneillon is the fourth in the order of Thrones, and tempts men with hatred against their enemies. (Adversary: Stephen.)

Second Hierarchy

Carreau, Prince of Powers, tempts men with hardness of heart. (Adversary: Vincent Ferrer.)

Carnivean is also a Prince of Powers, and does tempt men to obscenity and shamelessness. (Adversary: John the Evangelist.)

Oeillet is a Prince of Dominions. He tempts men to break the vow of poverty. (Adversary: Martin.)

Rosier is the second in the order of Dominions, and by his sweet and sugared words, he tempts men to fall in love. His adversary in heaven is Basil, who would not listen to amorous and enchanting language.

Verrier is Prince of Principalities, and tempts men against the vow of obedience, and makes the neck stiff and hard as iron, and incapable to stoop under the yoke of obedience. (Adversary: Bernard.)

Third Hierarchy

Belias, Prince of the order of Virtues, tempts men with arrogance. His adversary is Francis de Paul for his great and dove-like humility. He also tempts gentle-women to prank up [that is, dress up] themselves with new-fangled attires, to make wantons of their children, and to prattle unto them while Mass is saying, and so divert them from the service of God.

Olivier, Prince of the Archangels, tempts men with cruelty and mercilessness toward the poor. (Adversary: Lawrence.)

Aluvart is Prince of the Angels, but he is in another body (of another nun at Louviers) and hath not his abode here (in a Sister Madeleine, whom the exorcist Father Michaelis observed during her alleged diabolical possession at Aix-en-Provence).

Let us now continue with examples from Sacred Scripture that depict many different types of demons who operate in ways appropriate to their order:

Demons of Accusation

Then he showed me Joshua the high priest standing before the angel of the Lord, and Satan standing at his right hand to accuse him (Zech 3:1).

Demons of Condemnation

If anyone aspires to the office of bishop . . . He must not be a recent convert, or he may be puffed up with conceit and fall into the condemnation of the devil (1 Tm 3:1, 6).

Demons of Deafness

As they were going away, behold, a dumb demoniac was brought to him. And when the demon had been cast out, the dumb man spoke; and the crowds marvelled, saying, `Never was anything like this seen in Israel' (Mt 9:32-34).

Demons of Epilepsy

And when they came to the crowd, a man came up to him and kneeling before him said, `Lord, have mercy on my son, for he is an epileptic and he suffers terribly; for often he falls into the fire, and often into the water. And I brought him to your disciples, and they could not heal him.' And Jesus answered, `O faithless and persevering generation, how long am I to be with you? How long am I to bear with you? Bring him here to me.' And Jesus rebuked him, and the demon came out of him, and the boy was cured instantly (Mt 17:14-18).

Demons of Oppression

God anointed Jesus of Nazareth with the Holy Spirit and with power; he went about doing good and healing all that were oppressed by the devil, for God was with him" (Acts 10:38).

Demons of Possession

For fire will come upon her from the Everlasting for many days, and for a long time she will be inhabited by demons (Bar 4:35).

That evening, at sundown, they brought to him all who were sick or possessed with demons. And the whole city was gathered together about the door. And he healed many who were sick with various diseases, and cast out many demons; and he would not permit the demons to speak, because they knew him (Mk 1:32-34).

And the scribes who came down from Jerusalem said, `He is possessed by Beelzebub, and by the prince of demons he casts out the demons.' And he called them to him, and said to them in parables, `How can Satan cast out Satan? If a kingdom is divided against itself, that kingdom cannot stand. And if a house is divided against itself, that house will not be able to stand. And if Satan has risen up against himself and is divided, he cannot stand, but is coming to an end' (Mk 3:22-27).

So they went out and preached that men should repent. And they cast out many demons, and anointed with oil many that were sick and healed them (Mk 6:12-13).

John said to him, `Teacher, we saw a man casting out demons in your name, and we forbade him, because he was not following us.' But Jesus said, `Do not forbid him; for no one who does a mighty work in my name will be able soon after to speak evil of me. For he that is not against us is for us' (Mk 9:38-40).

And demons also came out of many, crying, `You are the Son of God!' But he rebuked them, and would not allow them to speak, because they knew that he was the Christ (Lk 4:41).

But if it is by the finger of God that I cast out demons, then the kingdom of God has come upon you (Lk 11:20).

At that very hour some Pharisees came, and said to him, `Get away from here, for Herod wants to kill you.' And he said to them, `Go and tell that fox, Behold, I cast out demons and perform cures today and tomorrow, and the third day I finish my course ' (Lk 13:31-32).

And the multitudes with one accord gave heed to what was said by Philip, when they heard him and saw the signs which he did. For unclean spirits came out of many who were possessed, crying with a loud voice; and many who were paralyzed or lame were healed (Acts 8:6-8).

Demons of Pride

If anyone aspires to the office of bishop . . . He must not be a recent convert, or he may be puffed up with conceit and fall into the condemnation of the devil (1 Tm 3:1, 6).

Therefore it says, `God opposes the proud, but gives grace to the humble.' Submit yourselves therefore to God. Resist the devil and he will flee from you (Jas 3:6-7).

Demons of Temptation

Then Jesus was led up by the Spirit into the wilderness to be tempted by the devil. And he fasted forty days and forty nights, and afterward he was hungry. And the tempter came and said to him, `If you are the Son of God, command these stones to become loaves of bread.' But he answered, `It is written, Man shall not live by bread alone, but by every word that proceeds from the mouth of God. ' Then the devil took him to the holy city, and set him on the pinnacle of the temple, and said to him, `If you are the Son of God, throw yourself down; for it is written, He will give his angels charge of you, and On their hands they will bear you up, lest you strike your foot against a stone. ' Jesus said to him, `Again it is written, You shall not tempt the Lord your God. ' Again, the devil took him to a very high mountain, and showed him all the kingdoms of the world and the glory of them; and he said to him, `All these I will give you, if you will fall down and worship me.' Then Jesus said to him, `Begone, Satan! for it is written, À ÀYou shall worship the Lord your God and him only shall you serve ' (Mt 4:1-10).

Demons of War and Destruction

Since therefore the children share in flesh and blood, he himself likewise partook of the same nature, that through death he might destroy him who has the power of death, that is, the devil, and deliver all those who through fear of death were subject to lifelong bondage (Heb 2:14-15).

Be sober, be watchful. Your adversary the devil prowls around like a roaring lion, seeking someone to devour (1 Pt 5:8).

For they are demonic spirits, performing signs, who go abroad to the kings of the whole world, to assemble them for battle on the great day of God the Almighty. . . . And they assembled them at the place which is called in Hebrew Armageddon (Rv 16:14, 16).

And when the thousand years are ended, Satan will be loosed from his prison and will come out to deceive the nations which are at the four corners of the earth, that is, Gog and Magog, to gather them for battle (Rv 20:8).

Demons Who Perform

Signs and Wonders

And I saw, issuing from the mouth of the dragon and from the mouth of the beast and from the mouth of the false prophet, three foul spirits like frogs; for they are demonic spirits, performing signs, who go abroad to the kings of the whole world, to assemble them for battle on the great day of God the Almighty (Rv 16:13-14).

The coming of the lawless one by the activity of Satan will be with all power and with pretended signs and wonders, and with all wicked deception for those who are to perish, because they refused to love the truth and so be saved (2 Thes 2:9-10).

For even Satan disguises himself as an angel of light (2 Cor 11:14).

Demons Who Encourage Sin

He who commits sin is of the devil; for the devil has sinned from the beginning. The reason the Son of God appeared was to destroy the works of the devil. No one born of God commits sin; for God's nature abides him, and he cannot sin because he is born of God. By this it may be seen who are the children of God, and who are the children of the devil: whoever does not do right is not of God, nor he who does not love his brother (1 Jn 3:8-10).

Individual Demons Versus Legions

What evidence from the Scriptures do we have to support the fact that multiple demons can simultaneously oppress or possess a victim? There are a number of New Testament cases that express this fact. In the Gospel of Matthew, Jesus enters the land of the Gerasenes near Galilee and meets a man who had demons (Mt 8:27). After Jesus asked the demon for its name, the reply was chilling: Legion (Mt 8:30), for many demons had entered him (Mt 8:30). Jesus exorcised the demons, and then they took up their abode in a herd of swine (Mt 8:33).

We see further evidence in the continued story of Jesus' encounter with the multiply possessed man of the Gerasenes: Then people went out to see what had happened, and they came to Jesus, and found the man from whom the demons had gone, sitting at the feet of Jesus, clothed and in his right mind; and they were afraid. And those who had seen it told them how he who had been possessed with demons was healed (Lk 8:35-36).

The Gospel of Matthew records the same story, with these words from the possessing spirits themselves: And behold, they cried out, `What have you to do with us, O Son of God? Have you come here to torment us before the time?' (Mt 8:29).

In Mark's Gospel, the story of multiple demons occurs in the life of Mary Magdalene: À ÀNow when he rose early on the first day of the week, he appeared first to Mary Magdalene, from whom he had cast out seven demons (Mk 16:9).

Another story from Luke's Gospel may or may not imply that individuals were possessed by a multitude of demons: And the twelve were with him, and also some women who had been healed of evil spirits and infirmities (Lk 8:2). This verse could imply that different women were infected by individual demons; yet the following verse gives the example of Mary Magdalene and her seven demons. Indeed, the Evangelist claims that demons were in control of many others (Lk 8:3).

Quarrelsome Spirits

Have nothing to do with stupid, senseless controversies; you know that they breed quarrels. And the Lord's servant must not be quarrelsome but kindly to everyone, an apt teacher, forbearing, correcting his opponents with gentleness. God may perhaps grant that they will repent and come to know the truth, and they may escape from the snare of the devil, after being captured by him to do his will (2 Tm 2:23-26).

Sacrifice to Demons

They sacrificed to demons which were no gods, to gods they had never known, to new gods that had come in of late, whom your fathers had never dreaded (Dt 32:17).

They sacrificed their sons and their daughters to the demons; they poured out innocent blood, the blood of their sons and daughters, whom they sacrificed to the idols of Canaan; and the land was polluted with blood (Ps 106:37).

 For you provoked him who made you, by sacrificing to demons and not to God (Bar 4:7). I imply that what pagans sacrifice they offer to demons and not to God. I do not want you to be partners with demons. You cannot drink the cup of the Lord and the cup of the demons. You cannot partake of the table of the Lord and the table of the demons (1 Cor 10:20-21).

Spirits of Aggression

But the evil spirit answered them, `Jesus I know, and Paul I know; but who are you?' And the man in whom the evil spirit was, leaped on them, mastered all of them, and overpowered them, so that they fled out of that house naked and wounded (Acts 19:15-16).

Spirits of Anger

Therefore, put away falsehood, let every one speak the truth with his neighbor, for we are members one of another. Be angry but do not sin; do not let the sun go down on your anger, and give no opportunity to the devil (Eph 4:25-27).

Rejoice then, O heaven and you that dwell therein! But woe to you, O earth and sea, for the devil has come down to you in great wrath, because he knows that his time is short! (Rv 12:12).

Then the devil was angry with the woman, and went off to make war on the rest of her offspring, on those who keep the commandments of God and bear testimony to Jesus (Rv 12:17).

Spirits of Betrayal

`Did I not choose you, the twelve, and one of you is a devil?'
He spoke of Judas the son of Simon Iscariot, for he, one of the
twelve, was to betray him (Jn 6:70-71).

And during the supper, when the devil had already put it into
the heart of Judas Iscariot, Simon's son, to betray him, Jesus,
knowing that the Father had given all things into his hands,
and that he had come from God and was going to God, rose
from supper, laid aside his garments, and girded himself with
a towel (Jn 13:2-4).

Spirits of Confusion

The ones along the path are those who have heard; then the
devil comes and takes away the words from their hearts, that
they may not believe and be saved (Lk 8:12).

Spirits of Deception

Now the Spirit expressly says that in later times some will
depart from the faith by giving heed to deceitful spirits and
doctrines of demons (1 Tm 4:1).

If anyone aspires to the office of bishop, he desires a noble
task. He must not be a recent convert, or he may be puffed up

with conceit and fall into the condemnation of the devil; moreover he must be well thought of by outsiders, or he may fall into reproach and the snare of the devil (1 Tm 3:1, 6-7).

And the great dragon was thrown down, that ancient serpent, who is called the Devil and Satan, the deceiver of the whole world (Rv 12:9).

You son of the devil, you enemy of all righteousness, full of all deceit and villainy, will you not stop making crooked the straight paths of the Lord? (Acts 13:10).

For even Satan disguises himself as an angel of light (2 Cor 11:14).

Spirits of Destruction

On the same day, at Ecbatana in Media, it also happened that Sarah, the daughter of Raguel, was reproached by her father's maids, because she had been given to seven husbands, and the evil demon Asmodeus had slain each of them before he had been with her as his wife (Tb 3:7-8).

Spirits of Frustration

But since we were bereft of you, brethren, for a short time, in person not in heart, we endeavored the more eagerly and with great desire to see you face to face; because we wanted to come to you I, Paul, again and again but Satan hindered us (1 Thes 2:17-18).

Spirits of Greed

A man named Ananias with his wife Sapphira sold a piece of property, and with his wife's knowledge he kept back some of the proceeds, and brought only a part and laid it at the apostles' feet. But Peter said, `Ananias, why has Satan filled your heart to lie to the Holy Spirit and to keep back part of the proceeds of the land? While it remained unsold, did it not remain your own? And after it was sold, was it not at your disposal? How is it that you have contrived this deed in your heart? You have not lied to men but to God' (Acts 5:1-4).

Then Satan answered the Lord, `Does Job fear God for naught? Hast thou not put a hedge about him and his house and all that he has, on every side? Thou hast blessed the work of his hands, and his possessions have increased in the land. But put forth thy hand now, and touch all that he has, and he will curse thee to thy face.' And the Lord said to Satan, `Behold, all that he has is in your power; only upon himself do not put forth your hand' (Jb 1:9-12).

Spirits of Jealousy

But through the devil's envy death entered the world (Wis 2:24).

This wisdom is not such that comes down from above, but is earthly, unspiritual, devilish. For where jealousy and selfish ambition exist, there will be disorder and every vile practice (Jas 3:16-16).

Spirits of Lust

Reports dating back to the early Church Fathers describe a type of spirit that sexually attacks a male or female. It was often believed that a malevolent spirit could take on a human form and rape its victim. A demon that attacks a female is known as an **incubus** (plural: **incubi**). Likewise, a demon that rapes a male is known as a **succubus** (plural: **succubi**). The incubus is known by a variety of names in other cultures: **follet** (French), **alp** (German), **duende** (Spanish), and **folletto** (Italian).

Many victims have described the physical appearance of the incubus. It can take on either a male or female shape. Sometimes the demon appears as a full-grown man, and other times it appears to be a young, handsome boy. Others have seen the incubus in the form of a rank goat, especially those who had dabbled in witchcraft.

During the Middle Ages, reports of alleged incubus and succubus attacks were at an all-time high. It was claimed that women were more licentious than men, especially since so many of them had taken to witchcraft and devil worship; thus, reports of incubus attacks (male demons who assault females) outnumbered the reports of succubi by about 9 to 1. Although it was well-known that a demonic spirit was neither male or female, nevertheless legends described the demons as taking on a bodily form in order to interact with human beings.

One of the great Doctors of the Church, St. Augustine of Hippo (354-430), described the incubus as a À Àdevil who injures women, desiring and acting carnally with them (De Trinitate).

Again from De Trinitate, St. Augustine makes this statement: Devils do indeed collect human semen, by means of which they are able to produce bodily effects; but this cannot be done without some local movement, therefore devils can transfer the semen which they have collected and inject it into the bodies of others.

Another great Doctor of the Church, St. Thomas Aquinas (1225-1274), made the following observation: If sometimes children are born from intercourse with demons, this is not because of the semen emitted by them, nor from the bodies they have assumed, but through the semen taken from some man for this purpose, seeing that the same demon who acts as a succubus for a man becomes an incubus for a woman (Summa Theologica).

The Church Doctor St. Alphonsus de Liguori (1696-1787) had this to say about the demon of lust: Sin with a succubus or incubus is called bestiality; to which sin is added also malice against religion, sodomy, adultery, and incest (Theologia Moralis). This work was highly acclaimed, being approved by Pope Benedict XIV (1740-1758).

St. Bernard of Clairvaux (1090-1153), Doctor of the Church, told a story that occurred to him in Nantes, France, during the year 1135. This story was recorded in the Sancti Bernardi Vita Secunda. At that time, a woman of the community sought his help. Bernard claims that the woman had been attacked by an incubus for six years. In the seventh year her husband, thinking she was committing adultery, divorced her. The pious saint advised the young woman to sleep with her ex-husband's staff on her bed, and to use it to fight off the demon whenever he appeared. After a series of prayers led by Bernard, the incubus troubled her no more.

Many of the saints have claimed to be attacked by incubi or succubi: among them St. Antony of Egypt (251-356), St. Hilary (d. 368), and St. Margaret of Cortona (1247-1297).

St. Athanasius (297-373), Doctor of the Church, once claimed that Antony's disciple, St. Hilary, was found lying down to sleep, encircled by naked women (Life of St. Antony). In this same work, it was said that St. Antony was attacked by a devil at night who threw filthy thoughts in his way and who imitated gestures of a naked woman.

In another documented case, it is claimed that St. Victorinus (d. 303), Bishop of Pettau, was seduced by an aggressive succubus.

Bishop Ermolaus of Verona (1453-1471) once wrote of a hermit who was a frequent victim of attacks by a succubus.

It is believed that St. Hippolytus (d. 235) once had an apparition of a naked woman. Fearing for his chastity, Hippolytus threw his chasuble over the apparition to conceal her nakedness. Immediately upon doing this, the vision turned into a corpse. Because of such visions, the fear of the succubus became enshrined in a famous Ambrosian hymn (Procul recedant somnia): Let all dreams and phantasms of the night . . . fade away, lest our bodies be polluted.

The Book of Jude gives witness to these spirits of lust: Now I desire to remind you, though you were once for all fully informed, that he who saved a people out of the land of Egypt, afterward destroyed those who did not believe. And the angels that did not keep their own position but left their proper dwelling have been kept by him in eternal chains in the nether gloom until the judgment of the great day; just as Sodom and Gomorrah and surrounding cities, while likewise acted immorally and indulged in unnatural lust, serve as an example by undergoing a punishment of eternal fire (Jude 5-7).

Spirits of Lying

You are of your father the devil, and your will is to do your father's desires. He was a murderer from the beginning, and has nothing to do with the truth, because there is no truth in him. When he lies, he speaks according to his own nature, for he is a liar and the father of lies (Jn 8:44).

Then the Lord said, `Who will entice Ahab, that he may go up and fall at Ramoth Gilead?' And one said one thing, and another said another. Then a spirit came forward and stood before the Lord, saying, `I will entice him.' And the Lord said to him, `By what means?' And he said, `I will go forth, and will be a lying spirit in the mouth of all his prophets' (1 Kgs 22:20-22).

Spirits of Seduction

So I would have younger widows marry, bear children, rule their households, and give the enemy no occasion to revile us. For some have already strayed after Satan (1 Tm 5:14-15).

But to the rest of you in Thyatira, who do not hold this teaching, who have not learned what some call the deep things of Satan, to you I say, I do not lay upon you any other burden; only hold fast what you have, until I come (Rv 2:24-25).

Spirits of Wickedness

For we are not contending against flesh and blood, but against the principalities, against the powers, against the world rulers of this present darkness, against the spiritual hosts of wickedness in the heavenly places (Eph 6:12).

Spirits Who Deceive Nations

And he seized the dragon, that ancient serpent, who is the Devil and Satan, and bound him for a thousand years, and threw him into the pit, and shut it and sealed it over him, that he should deceive the nations no more, till the thousand years were ended (Rv 20:2-3).

And the devil who had deceived them was thrown into the lake of fire and brimstone where the beast and the false prophet were, and they will be tormented day and night for ever and ever (Rv 20:10).

Worship of Demons

The rest of mankind, who were not killed by these plagues, did not repent of the works of their hands nor give up worshiping demons and idols of gold and silver and bronze and stone and wood, which cannot either see or hear or walk; nor did they repent of their murders or their sorceries or their immorality or their thefts (Rv 9:20-21).

Activities Of The Evil Spirit

Poltergeist Phenomena

Of all the activities associated with demonic spirits, perhaps none is more familiar or frightening than poltergeist phenomena. **Poltergeist** comes from the German word for noisy ghost. Such activity has often been called poltergeist disturbance, and the entire collection of such phenomena is known as **poltergeistery**.

Poltergeist activity has been reported around the world throughout recorded history. Before the 1960s, this phenomenon was not studied scientifically, nor was the documentation as extensive as today. Even so, prior to that time there have been some 375 cases reported around the world: England reported 127; France, 58; the United States, 56; Germany, 29; with the remainder scattered throughout the rest of the world, including Canada, India, Russia, Spain, Chile, and Greece.

As early as 335 A.D., Jacob Grimm wrote about a poltergeist that bombarded a house with stones that came through the walls. This was explained in detail in the work Deutsche Mythologie. Later on, in the Bibliotheca Rerum Germanicarum, another case was reported that explained the phenomena of spontaneous fires ignited by unseen forces and objects that appeared out of nowhere. By the Middle Ages, such reports increased dramatically.

Even though some of these cases are hundreds of years old, it is interesting to note that such experiences are mainly from developed or civilized countries. This observation is important, for it disproves the theory that only uncivilized and primitive cultures are susceptible to such trickery or superstition.

One of most common means of triggering poltergeist phenomena has been through the use of Ouija boards and participation in seances. The **seance**, a form of table-turning, is conducted with various people who sit around a table and attempt to communicate with the dead. One known as a **medium** is employed to serve as the communicator, or one who makes contact with the departed spirit. The entire activity involves the occult practice known as **spiritism**, which is forbidden by most major religions.

The first known case of spiritism in America was reported in March of 1848 in the state of New York. Soon after, the practice had spread throughout Europe. Originally, spiritism was known as **spiritualism**.

The danger with such activities is that one never knows exactly what type of spirit will respond. Unfortunately, many are falsely convinced that they communicate with departed loved ones when in fact they have opened the door to diabolical infiltration. That is why the Scriptures themselves forbid the dabbling with such practices: There shall not be found among you anyone who burns his son or his daughter as an offering, anyone who practices divination, a **soothsayer**, or an **augur**, or a **sorcerer**, or a **charmer**, or a **medium**, or a **wizard**, or a **necromancer**. For whoever does these things is an abomination to the Lord (Dt 18:10-12).

Serious investigation into poltergeist activity is usually reserved for parapsychologists, who also study the following experiences: **mental telepathy** (the communication between two minds by means other than the normal sensory channel); **telekinesis** or **psychokinesis** (the movement of physical objects through the power of the mind); **clairvoyance** (the ability to perceive things not in sight); **psychic impulses** (insights caused through energy released by electrical discharges in the air and in the mind); etc.

Most parapsychologists see three potential sources for poltergeist activity: those that occur through the psychic powers of an individual (the most commonly acknowledged type), those that occur because of departed spirits or ghosts, and those activities associated with diabolical phenomena.

Poltergeist activity is normally associated with the ability of the mind to manipulate the environment. Usually, the poltergeist phenomenon occurs with a single individual in a household. Statistically, this individual is usually a child or adolescent, and it is more common with girls than with boys. Parapsychologists have thought that the emotional and mental crisis that goes with the age of puberty contributes to the onslaught of poltergeist activity, as if the phenomenon becomes an unleashing of psychic powers.

Although many feel that such activity may result through **departed spirits** or **ghosts**, nevertheless distinct demonic phenomena have been identified with some poltergeist disturbances. These activities are so well-known among demonologists and parapsychologists alike that both fields of discipline treat demonic disturbances as realities within the supernatural or preternatural world.

In order to better understand poltergeist phenomena, perhaps it would be appropriate here to describe the various ways these spirits affect the physical environment around them.

It is often stated that the major difference between hauntings and poltergeist activities is this: A **haunting** (normally attributed to a ghost or departed spirit) infests places, whereas a poltergeist infests either places or people. Most in the scientific community believe that a poltergeist is only a ghost; those in theological circles contend that it is none other than a diabolical spirit. Another difference is noted: While hauntings seems to occur over long periods of time indeed, they may go on for years; poltergeist activity is usually of short but intense duration.

Diabolical Apparitions

Apparitions are appearances or visions from the spiritual world. These appearances normally take the form of human shapes or entities, although apparitions of animals are not uncommon experiences. There are **ghostly apparitions** (those of departed human spirits), **heavenly apparitions** (those that appear as Jesus, the heavenly angels, or the saints), and **diabolical apparitions** (images or forms perceived by the mind and caused by the activity of the evil spirit). Sometimes heavenly apparitions are known as **supernatural apparitions**, while demonic appearances are called **preternatural apparitions**.

The question often posed by the faithful is this: Are they one and the same? In other words, are all apparitions from a heavenly or diabolical source? It must be admitted that many seriously doubt the belief in **earthbound spirits** or **departed spirits**: the so-called ghosts of horror movies and literature.

Yet we all acknowledge that man is given an eternal spirit that leaves his physical body at the moment of death. Does the human spirit or the soul to some arrive in heaven or hell instantaneously upon death? Are some spirits allowed to momentarily remain on earth, or can they come back for some reason that we are not yet prepared to know? What about the numerous reports of Catholics who have claimed to see apparitions of souls from purgatory who appear to implore their aid through prayers or good works? And these reports are well-documented; dozens of these experiences are claimed by the saints themselves. Are these not types of departed spirits that are neither diabolical nor heavenly? These are difficult questions to answer; to believe in all types of spirits may or may not be in line with the truth. But no human knows everything about the spiritual world. Perhaps it is best to keep an open mind to all these possibilities in order to be prepared for any experience that we might encounter. It may sound silly as a Catholic to presume that ghosts really exist. Some will simply say that the idea of ghosts is just another superstitious fantasy of the mind. Yet one has to answer the questions about the souls in purgatory mentioned previously. How does one account for those experiences that occur through the lips of credible sources? Such poltergeist attacks have been mentioned in the writings of such saints as John Vianney (1786-1859), Teresa of Avila (1515-1582), Benedict (480-547), and Martin of Tours (316-397).

For now, let us limit our study to the poltergeist experience caused by demonic spirits. Besides the apparitions as noted above, another phenomenon involves what is known as **teleportation**. During the outbreak of the poltergeist attack, household objects have been known to disappear and then reappear elsewhere in the same house. Most often, these objects turn up in unexpected places; frequently, they have been seen to drop from the ceiling. At other times, physical objects disappear and are never seen again.

Religious objects are particular targets for the diabolical spirit. If a crucifix is hanging on the wall, it may be turned upside down or thrown to the ground. A sheet may be placed over the crucified image in order to hide its appearance. This is a true sign of a diabolical spirit infesting the home.

In a poltergeist-infected home, objects may move about the house with strange trajectories that seem to defy the laws of gravity. Bottles may explode, objects slide across shelves, appliances turn on by themselves, etc. A strange phenomenon involves rocks, bolts, or nuts that appear to fall on the roof of the house. Many have witnessed falling rocks bombarding the inside of the home as well.

In the infested home, **de-materializations** and **deportations** may occur. The former involves objects that suddenly disappear from a particular location. The latter occurs when objects appear out of nowhere and in a particular place or room.

A particularly strange type of **materialization** is often reported at demonically infested sites. This involves the spontaneous appearance of **apports**: solid or liquid substances that are often hard to identify but that appear from no identifiable source. In some cases, the substance is sticky; in others, a foul odor or stench is emitted from the strange, foreign object. If these experiences are true, then it is obvious that the human mind alone cannot be responsible for such acts of nature.

In many poltergeist cases, reports of **spontaneous fires** are common. These fires are thought to be caused by a malevolent or demonic spirit, for other destructive acts are often associated with this experience. In such cases, **infestation** may lead to **diabolical oppression**.

It has been reported that biting marks, lacerations, and skin wounds are often inflicted on a particular victim of the poltergeist. These marks appear without any visible signs of origin: No person is seen to inflict such wounds on the victim.

It must be acknowledged that many skin conditions are caused by psychological or neurological disorders. Yet in these cases, there is no doubt that the severity of the wounds could not be caused by such disorders alone.

Is it really true that such strange phenomena are caused by inhuman demonic spirits? In many of these cases, it is obvious that a **preternatural intelligence** is behind each and every act. These actions seem to target particular people and are designed for harm or destruction. Fear and confusion are often felt by the victim of such actions. The bizarre phenomenon usually gets progressively worse or more intense as time moves along.

But the obvious sign of diabolical activity is the attacks upon anything with a religious connotation: holy objects such as crucifixes, relics of the saints, Bibles, and prayers. Oftentimes, a priest involved in the investigation becomes the object of a direct and malicious attack. These cases are so numerous that their documentation cannot be denied.

Demonic poltergeist activity is a type of phenomenon usually associated with the phases of diabolical attack known as infestation, infiltration, or oppression. Indeed, many similarities exist between the parapsychological observations of poltergeist phenomena and those of the demonologist.

For further references concerning diabolic poltergeists, the following sources might be of interest: Michel de Saint Pierre's The Remarkable Curay of Ars; Monsignor Leon Cristiani' Evidence of Satan in the Modern World; Father John J. Nicola's Diabolic Possession and Exorcism; Father Herbert Thurston's Ghosts and Poltergeists; and Father Carl Vogl's Begone Satan: A Soul-Stirring Account of Diabolical Possession.

Books of the Bible
(In Alphabetical Order)

Old Testament

1 Chr / 1 Chronicles
2 Chr / 2 Chronicles
1 Kgs / 1 Kings
2 Kgs / 2 Kings
1 Mc / 2 Maccabees
1 Mc / 2 Maccabees
1 Sm / 1 Samuel
2 Sm / 2 Samuel
Am / Amos
Bar / Baruch
Dn / Daniel
Dt / Deuteronomy
Eccl / Ecclesiastes
Est / Esther
Ex / Exodus
Ez / Ezekiel
Ezr / Ezra
Gn / Genesis
Hb / Habakkuk
Hg / Haggai
Hos / Hosea
Is / Isaiah
Jer / Jeremiah
Jb / Job
Jl / Joel
Jon / Jonah
Jos / Joshua
Jgs / Judges

Jdt / Judith
Lam / Lamentations
Lv / Leviticus
Mal / Malachi
Mi / Micah
Na / Nahum
Neh / Nehemiah
Nm / Numbers
Ob / Obadiah
Prv / Proverbs
Ps(s) / Psalms
Ru / Ruth
Sir / Sirach
Sg / Song of Solomon
Tb / Tobit
Wis / Wisdom
Zec / Zechariah
Zep / Zephaniah

New Testament

1 Cor / 2 Corinthians
1 Cor / 2 Corinthians
1 Jn / 1 John
2 Jn / 2 John
3 Jn / 3 John
1 Pt / 1 Peter
2 Pt / 2 Peter
1 Thes / 1 Thessalonians
2 Thes / 2 Thessalonians
1 Tm / 1 Timothy
2 Tm / 2 Timothy
Acts / Acts of the Apostles
Col / Colossians
Eph / Ephesians

Gal / Galatians
Heb / Hebrews
Jas / James
Lk / Luke
Mk / Mark
Mt / Matthew
Phlm / Philemon
Phil / Philippians
Rom / Romans
Rv / Revelation
Ti / Titus

If you found this book to be informative, please leave a comment! Just go to the bottom of the following page link to express your thoughts. Thanks!

http://www.amazon.com/gp/product/B01A5MP9GC?*Version* =1&*entries*=0

My other published ebooks are on my Amazon Author Central page:

http://www.amazon.com/-/e/B001KIZJS4

Printed in Great Britain
by Amazon